Traveling Through Glass

Also by Lisa Harris

Fiction

'Geechee Girls

Allegheny Dream

The Raven's Tale

Boxes

Low Country Stories

Traveling Through Glass

poetry by Lisa Harris
artwork by Patricia Brown

Cayuga Lake Books
Ithaca, New York

Traveling Through Glass
Poetry by Lisa Harris
Artwork by Patricia Brown

Copyright © 2017 by Lisa Harris
All rights reserved

Copyright © 2017 by Patricia Brown
All rights reserved

First Printing – December 2017
ISBN: 978-1-68111-210-7
Library of Congress Control Number: 2017960356
Cover Art and All Drawings by Patricia Brown

NO PART OF THIS BOOK MAY BE REPRODUCED IN ANY FORM,
BY PHOTOCOPYING OR BY ANY ELECTRONIC OR MECHANICAL
MEANS, INCLUDING INFORMATION STORAGE OR RETRIEVAL
SYSTEMS, WITHOUT PERMISSION IN WRITING FROM THE
COPYRIGHT OWNER/AUTHOR

Printed in the U.S.A.

0   1   2   3   4   5

Front cover: 10 Spirit, 2017, acrylic on canvas, 36 x 48 inches

Back cover: 1 Shalom, 2017, acrylic on canvas, 24 x 30 inches

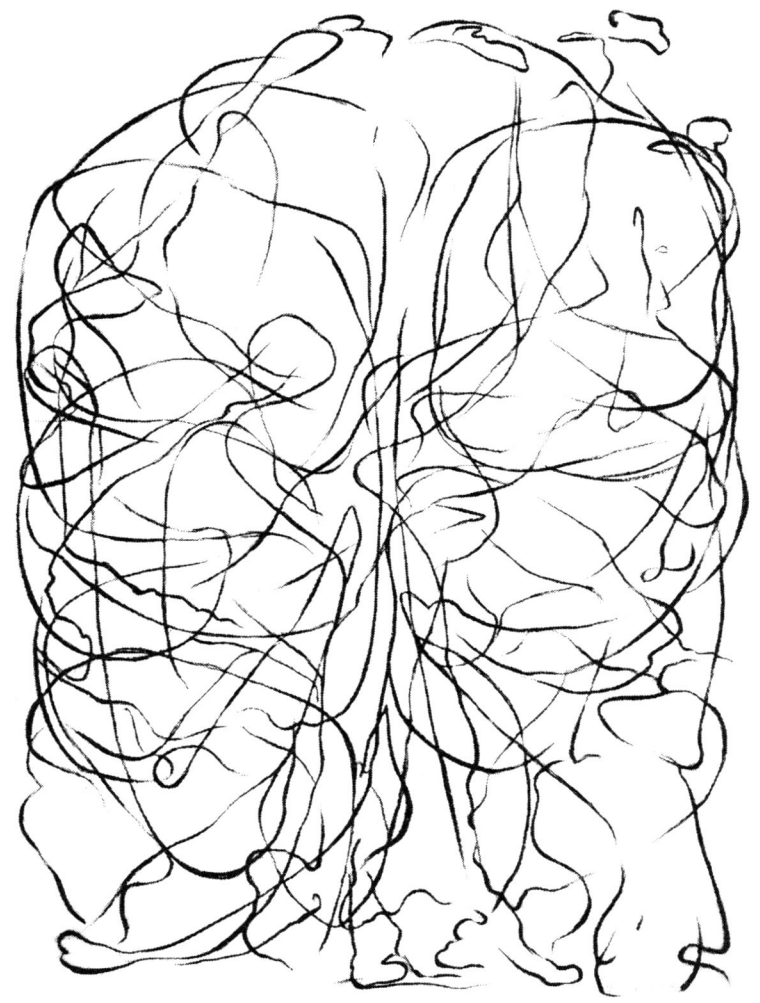

10 Spirit, 2016, charcoal on paper, 22 x 30 inches

for Joan B. and Glenn E. Shope
guardians and guides

for JSS
always

for Louis Hicks
a center in Time and Motion

for Zama Eng
boundless friend

CONTENTS

I. Counting 1

    Nothing and Everything 3

    Shalom 5

    Balance 9

    Family 13

    House 17

    Change 21

    Connection 25

    Blood 29

    Eternity 33

    Patience 37

    Spirit 41

    Knowing 43

    Complete 45

II. Breathing 47

III. Seeking 59

    Holding Half 61

    In This Moment 65

    Synesthesia 67

    Salt and Light ~ A Covenant 68

    Extravagant Mercy 74

Mending..75
Practice..77
Raw 79

I.
Counting

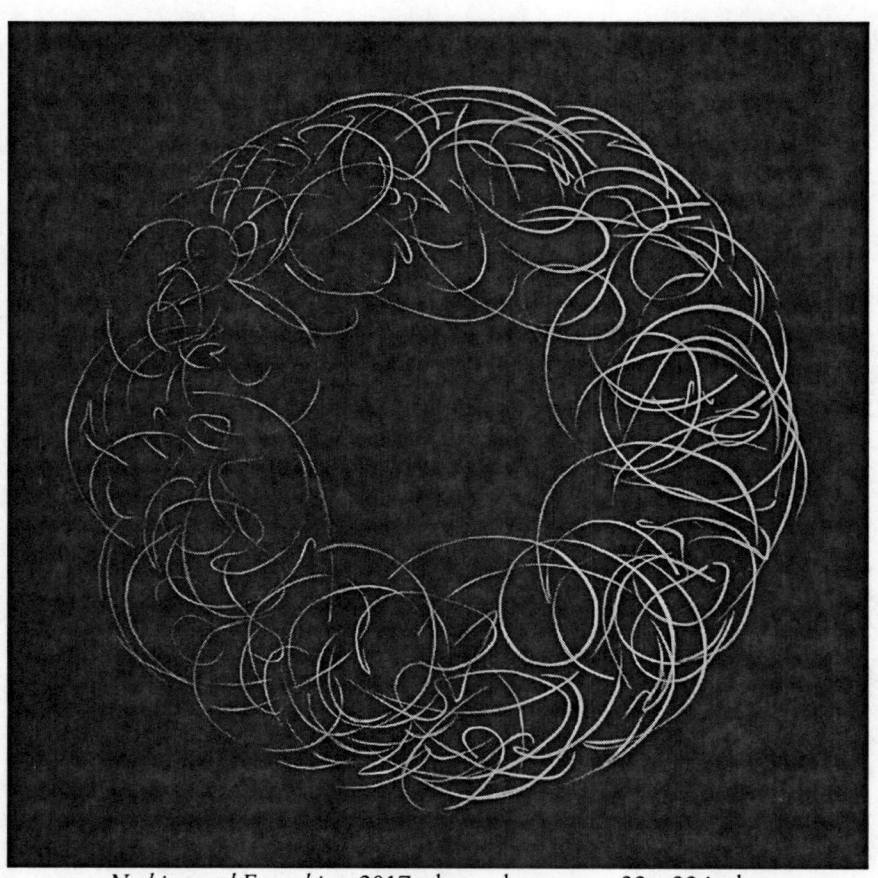

Nothing and Everything, 2017, charcoal on paper, 22 x 22 inches

0

Nothing and Everything

Zero holds a place of absence, a mid-point between plus one and minus one. Look closely at a pie, a cake, a world—things we cut up. Once made, they cannot be enlarged, but they can be shared in different parts, in different pieces, in different chunks. Time, amorphous and precise, teases us as it stretches beyond us, measures us by ticks and tocks, speaking a language of ticking and tocking. We are zero—a place of absence and presence, a mid-point between eternity and before now. We set time traps, for each other and for ourselves. We call them deadlines, milestones, anniversaries, paydays, Sabbaths, birthdays, national holidays, elections, weekends, and funerals. Zero, naught, zilch, zip, aught: we leave and never arrive, as Zeno predicted, reductio ad absurdum, whenever we reach where we have been, we still have farther to go, no tortoise needed in this race, absurdly running and never arriving until Death reaches out and snatches us. Prior to that moment, we are arrows—in a motionless moment—fixed on a spinning point called time.

Shalom, 2016, charcoal on paper, 22 x 30 inches

1

Shalom

First principle: Perfection, peace, wholeness, being complete:
    one.

We speak into each other's lives and begin becoming.
Tenor toned your velvet voice makes a pillow for me to choose.

When I misunderstand or don't hear, I trust timbre
and pitch. I trust you. On a campus where we met,
I heard your voice above others, heard it before I saw

you approaching—and you are easy to spot at a distance,
or in a crowd. Not loud. Present. Tall, strong, able
to fell a tree, haul rock, split logs, drag deer, lift me—
as essential to me as hydrogen, atomic number 1, is to star
    formation.

Our love is water and makes up 60 percent of each of us.
Our love provides stores of hydrogen to keep us young.
Hydrogen, the lightest element, instigates positive energy,
abundant in us and in stars. Without it, no water and no sun.
You are my only-est one, my true companion.

The first person to enter a house on the first day
of the new year in Viet Nam, and elsewhere, sets
a blessing or a curse, so each house invites
a best person, one who has power to create well-being.
You are the blessing in my house—day by day.
I invite you. I open myself to you. I let you in.

You enter. You open your heart. You surround me
in your arms, speak in silent kisses, hold me tight,
and hold me loose. You encourage wild, insist on free.
Entirety. One is the number of our sun,
of what is best, of yet to come, of unity, of God
in us, wonder and hope, creation and growth.

First principle: truth, light, shadow and spirit: one.

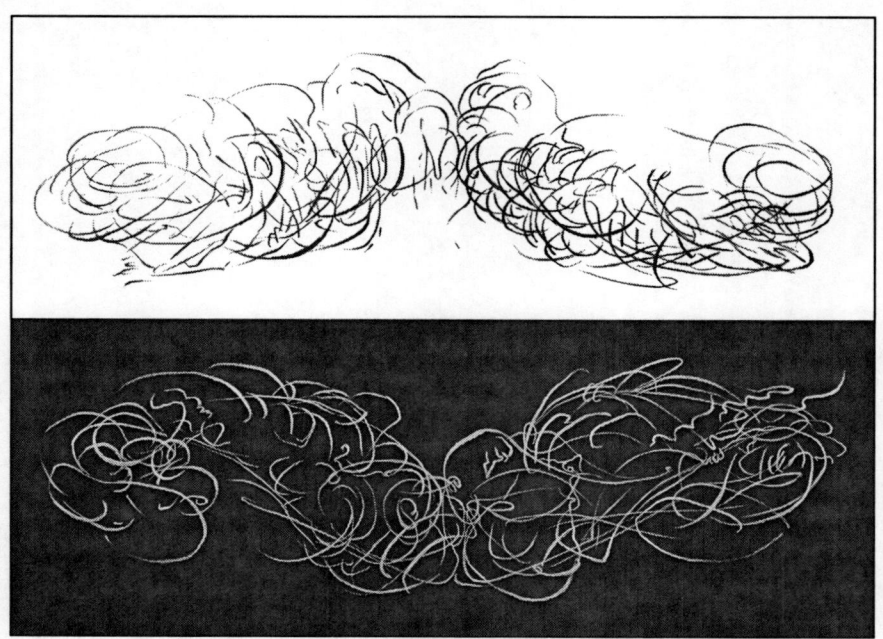

Balance, 2017, charcoal on paper, 30 x 22 inches

2

Balance

If two is too many, and one is too few, where is the balance
 between the two?
Two angels follow each person in life and write down good
 deeds and bad.

Two silver cords hold our souls to our bodies:
one linked to our brains and one linked to heaven.

If what we give, in turn becomes what we receive, is that
 justice?
She stands before us holding her scales, balanced and empty.

What if we unlearn opposites and duality as our primary frame
 of thought?
Our movements become joining, attracting, accepting, shifting
 and holding,

then letting go to the sound of two silver trumpets ordered by
 God
and made by Moses. Is their sound harmony? And to what are
 we called?

An eye for an eye, a tooth for a tooth is, after all, reciprocal—
and reductive. I will keep my eye and tooth; you keep yours.

If division is independence, is connecting imprisonment?
If we flip these, are they not also true? Connecting frees and
 dividing captures.

Two mattes frame two pears painted on a purple tray.
Two eyes watch and two hands touch, both insufficient and
    too much.

And lovers who yearn even after years together, crave smell
    and touch
to feel alive, rip open pomegranates and gasp at ruby seeds,
    too many to count.

Family, 2016, charcoal on paper, 22 x 30 inches

3

Family

Three could be small for a family, if the family were isolated and
   closed.
But if a family of three weaves itself into a larger fabric, three is
   perfect,
just like the number's mystery; three is wholeness. After all,

a triangle is the most stable shape. Ask an engineer, an
   architect, a designer.
Think in threes: beginning, middle, end; birth, life, death;
   one, two, three
and many, the way the ancient ones counted. Think:
   unfold, maintain, conclude.

Proportions shift, gain, and lose: three wishes, three weird
   sisters, three crosses
on a hill—two thieves and a third who stole our hearts and
   saved us.
Three virtues: faith, hope, and love. Three treasures:
   mirror, sword and jewel—

another way to name truth, courage and compassion.
To tell the truth, we must begin by looking at ourselves.
To locate courage, we must carry the double-edged sword

of truth and kindness. With the strength of these, we make a
   diamond cut
of multifaceted compassion. Hindu philosophers tell us
   there are
three attributes occurring at all times: sattva, rajas, and tamas—

goodness and peaceful virtue; passion and action; destruction
and chaos.
White light, red passion, and the darkest dark—when balanced,
they spark
us to ignite a life of responsibility. We merge and mix to
expand.

As humans, we perceive three dimensions: heaven, earth and
hell.
We have three primary colors: red, blue and yellow, and from
them,
we can create all the others, tint by tint, and shade by shade.

Our tri-chromatic retina contains three types of color receptors.
Our friend, the octopus, has three hearts, and each cat has a
third eyelid.
Our best philosophers created tri-chotomies to absolve us of
absolutes.

So, on the count of three, "One. Two. Three!" Let us begin to
love
again. We have spent more than our three nights in the belly of
the whale.
We have been tempted at least three times by our combined
worst thoughts.

The energy we put out into the world will be returned to us
three times.
So, on the count of three, "One. Two. Three!" Let us forgive
and laugh
again. Permanent good thoughts, sweetness of tongue, and
benevolence.

House, 2016, charcoal on paper, 22 x 30 inches

4

House

A square, a cross, and four directions place us in space and
 make us stable.
We are fixed in a stillness that draws our energy in.
Seeking a haven, we read signs and symbols silently.
We want a house to hold us the way we hold each other:
 tight and loose.

Loose and tight we hold and release, release and hold.
Your knee brushes against my elbow, my cheekbone rests
 upon your brow.
Buddhists say our beloved is our house.
At a recent dinner party guests complimented our meal.

"This gumbo is delicious, and the bouquet smells sweet."
You nod and say, "My house made this gumbo. My house
 gathered
this bouquet from flowers she grew in her garden."
We are each other's house. We are blessed in this way.

We dwell in the heart of our true love: in cold and heat,
in joy and grief, in feast and famine, and together we make
 a house.
We ignore life's four sore judgments: war, famine, wild beasts
 and pestilence
when we can. We vote our conscience and hold hands.

Grace sings of miracles, wonders, signs and gifts.
I watch as you push blades against grass,
rake against leaves, brush against wall, and pull
me into the house your arms make.

Her house and his house. Our house.
We think all things four: Four gospels, four points on a
    compass
and on a cross, four quarters in a dollar, four chambers
in our pounding hearts. Imagine quaking stars and raging seas,

galaxies made of glass, hummingbirds and buzzing bees
announcing our relocation, arriving in the present by returning
    home.

Change, 2016, charcoal on paper, 22 x 30 inches

5

Change

Cosmic ray spallation and supernovae produce boron,
whose atomic number is 5. Plants need it to strengthen
their fibers; humans need it to strengthen their bones,
to lessen the crack and the crumble! Boron arrives to Earth
in scarce amounts, ejected when a ray particle

collides with matter—expelling nucleons from the object hit.
Who could see it coming? How could anyone prepare?
Oh! We weren't there for boron's primordial birth, and
neither was boron, without a conscience, without a soul,
without a past like the worst among us.

Sets of 5: Islam's 5 Pillars, faith, prayer, chastity, fasting, pilgrimage;
western and eastern worlds insist on water earth air fire ether,
water fire earth wood metal; Ten Commandments
teach in two sets of five, first our relationship to god,
and then our relationship one to another.

Each set of 5 has the power to transmute, reform, transform.
Jews in the desert heard the voice of god,
"Make a sanctuary for me, and I will dwell among you."
So Moses took the blueprint and built a wilderness
tabernacle made of all things 5.

5 curtains, 5 bars, 5 pillars, 5 sockets, to build
the altar measured in 5 cubits—an ancient measure
the length of forearm to fingertip.
Eighteen inches, more or less, still used today
to determine intervals between stakes in hedgerows.

But I digress. God described holy anointing oil, too,
for the desert sanctuary: 5 ingredients in equal parts,
myrrh, cinnamon, calamus, cassia and oil,
mixed to soothe the mind and heal the heart in a place apart,
sanctified cubit by cubit, gate by gate, grain of sand by grain of sand.

Time travel next to the crucifixion and observe:
5 wounds inflicted in fear to kill our saviors, ourselves.
Scourged, crowned with thorns, nailed, wounded,
slashed with swords, making us as primordial as boron.
Each of us can only come to God on God's terms.

Last stop: 2 a.m. on a couch in a living room somewhere in America.
A woman shuffles a tarot deck, seeking insight while
she yearns to build a sanctuary in the desert of her dreams.
She lays the wheel of fortune pattern and draws all four 5s.
That says it all, she thinks. Change. For her outcome card,
she draws the sun.

Connection, 2017, charcoal on paper, 22 x 30 inches

6

Connection

If you believe it took six days to create the universe, you are not alone.
You are connected to an old story and all who have considered it.
You hang by a thread to a tale told over and over again.
Thou shalt not kill, the sixth commandment, in midrash considers gossip
as a weapon that kills. Watch how and when and where you use words.
The weave and the braid wrap truth, lies and fear into a formidable chain.

Imagine you are a bee living in a six-sided cell.
Your job is to carry nectar home to make it into honey.
Or what if you were part of a water crystal, a snowflake,
a prong on the Star of David—one sixth of an entirety?
Consider being blind and craving the connection formed
when others read the written word. Your fingertips become your eyes

as they trace and decode 6 dots placed in two columns of three dots each,
some raised, some lowered, a silent telegraphing to your heart and mind,
bringing letters into words, words into sentences, sentences into meaning.
You receive entire worlds. You stack and sort, merge and discard. And then,
you read the terrifying Norse myth of the Fenris wolf held tight by a leash

made of 6 things that no longer exist, braided now into a metal
    chain to bind him:

footfall of cats, beard of a woman, roots of a mountain,
long sinews of a bear, breath of a fish, and spit of a bird.
The Fenris wolf watches you with yellow eyes.
You feel its smooth sharp teeth around your wrist biting off
    your hand.
The thrust sword is now lodged in your throat. You are bound
    to a rock
until doomsday, when you had been hoping for a world without
    end.

Work, 2017, charcoal on paper, 22 x 30 inches

7

Blood

Where to begin? When she was 17, ten plus seven, in the
    7th month,
on the 7th day, she flew on a 747 above one of the 7 seas
    to one of the 7 continents.
At first, she did not notice patterns in what she saw
    as an endless life. But
she did notice frieze patterns in tile work on mosques
    —long lines of repeats—
patterns in clouds, and patterns in short words and lines
in a telegram that called her home. She saw reflections,
    cross wise
in the thick window glass. Clouds made glide patterns
    and half-turns.

She is the 7th daughter of the 7th daughter, but there is no
    blues song written
for her, no wailing man singing, no magic granted her
    when she throws dice
or asks for grace. She arrives too late to say goodbye. She cares
    and she does not care.
She knows how to walk 7 directions in beauty—north, east,
    south, west, up, down
and center—where she wants to dwell—beneath a turquoise
    sky, light footed
on red parched clay. She carries a candle before her,
    a stag walks behind her,
and raven wings fly out to her sides—balancing, balancing.

It has taken far more than 7 days to create herself,
    and she is still not finished.
She has merged the 7 rainbow colors into black,
    and in this 7th year,
she listens for the arrival of locusts. She hears pounding
    and counts
cycles of 7, as notes in a measure with an odd rhythm,
    her heart beat.
Raven hops, spin hops, jumps, sidles, steps,
    spin jumps and spin sidles,
practicing his 7 moves in a revolving pattern.
    What is spiritual symmetry?
What does it smell like—and the taste,
    would she need more salt?

She sleeps 7 hours, or is it 7 years, or 70? She has participated
    in 7 sins and lived,
was lost and found 7000 times, dead and reborn.
    When has she lived 7 virtues?
Once she was faithful to herself; once she was prudent;
    once she had courage;
once she was just; once she gave herself to herself.
    She can be humble; and
she understands that symmetry is evanescent,
a sheen of sweat that appears on her brow
    when she labors.
Hope, crimson and translucent, flows
    like blood in her veins.

Eternity, 2017, charcoal on paper, 22 x 30 inches

8

Eternity

Lay an 8 on its side and eternity looks back at you.
Envision an 8 on your body's trunk and breathe
    through the roadway you travel.
You are on a Mobius strip that loops and loops,
    a one-sided surface
with one boundary; travel it fully and never
    cross over the edge.
Welcome to the conveyor belt of life! Balance
    and motion are gifts in and
across time. You are provided for. You have all
    that you need. You belong
to infinity, larger than any number. You balance
    between worlds.
Join. Divide. Participate. Prosper. Focus:
    verbs you carry in a basket as reminders.

You are an eight-cylinder engine and you propel yourself,
    part spider part octopus,
during the night to the eighth realm where gods dwell—
    making webs to collect dew and flies,
dancing across the ocean floor and resting in the coral reefs.
    During the day, you transform into an eight-spotted
forester moth: your black wings glisten;
your white spots shimmer and glow.
                        You are forced to choose
who you will be, and so you pick, with some hope
and some regret, the order of cephalopod; you abandon

any desire for a skeleton because your greater wish
is to fit in and squeeze through tight spaces. Like a writer,
you disguise yourself by expelling ink
so you can jet away from danger.

You remember both now and long ago.
You know shapes and patterns, and you refuse
entanglement. You build your house from discarded
coconut shells and mostly live alone.
Each breath is a new beginning and a continuation.
You quaver and hover with strength and power
and refuse to tie yourself in knots
over loss and anger, over anticipation and fear.
You turn inward and become attentive.

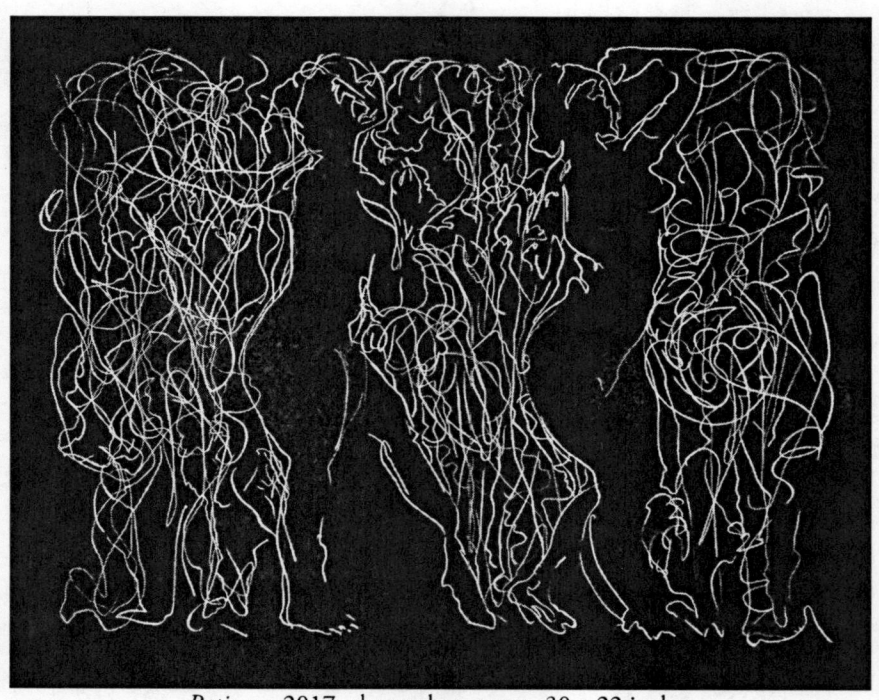

Patience, 2017, charcoal on paper, 30 x 22 inches

9

Patience

If a person does not understand a life-lesson, she must wait nine years to hear the voice of god calling, for her to learn. Nine years in god-time is short, but in human time it is long, until you have lived through it, and then it passes in the blink of an eye even while including drop-ins to heaven and the abyss. Three worlds exist—world of spirit, world of soul, world of matter: across and within them nine choruses of angels sing the night, through azure sky, across time's dull ticking. Their silken glass-edged voices vibrate in ether, diffuse in light, illuminate stars, and land like kisses on sun, moon, nature and the Milky Way.

9 months for human gestation, and 9 months to complete a compost cycle. 9 when spoken in Chinese sounds the same as "long-lasting." 9 circles in Dante's Hell, and how many have each of us dwelt in? Aztecs assigned 9 to Night and Earth's power and drew from both to live. There are 72 names for god, and 108 names for the Goddess: each number divisible by 9. 9 demands we eliminate cowardice, hesitation, and fixation on what we cannot change, 9 demands we fight superstition, prejudice, and empty conventions, 9 demands we choose health, embrace godly order, and become clear and clean.

In 1529, fluorine was described and given the atomic number 9 because of its protons. Flourine helped smelt metals, etch glass, augment fertilizers and herbicides, reduce cavities in teeth, aid in refrigeration, fight depression, raise blood pressure, and expedite humans waking from ether. It also burns away the ozone layer, and is used in the creation of nuclear bombs. Extremely reactive and explosive, fluorine resembles humans and humans resemble flourine. How do we balance and control it? How do we balance and control ourselves? If a person does not understand a life lesson, she is destined to repeat the mistake until she chooses a different path, where she walks and listens to God's voice above and within turbulence and silence.

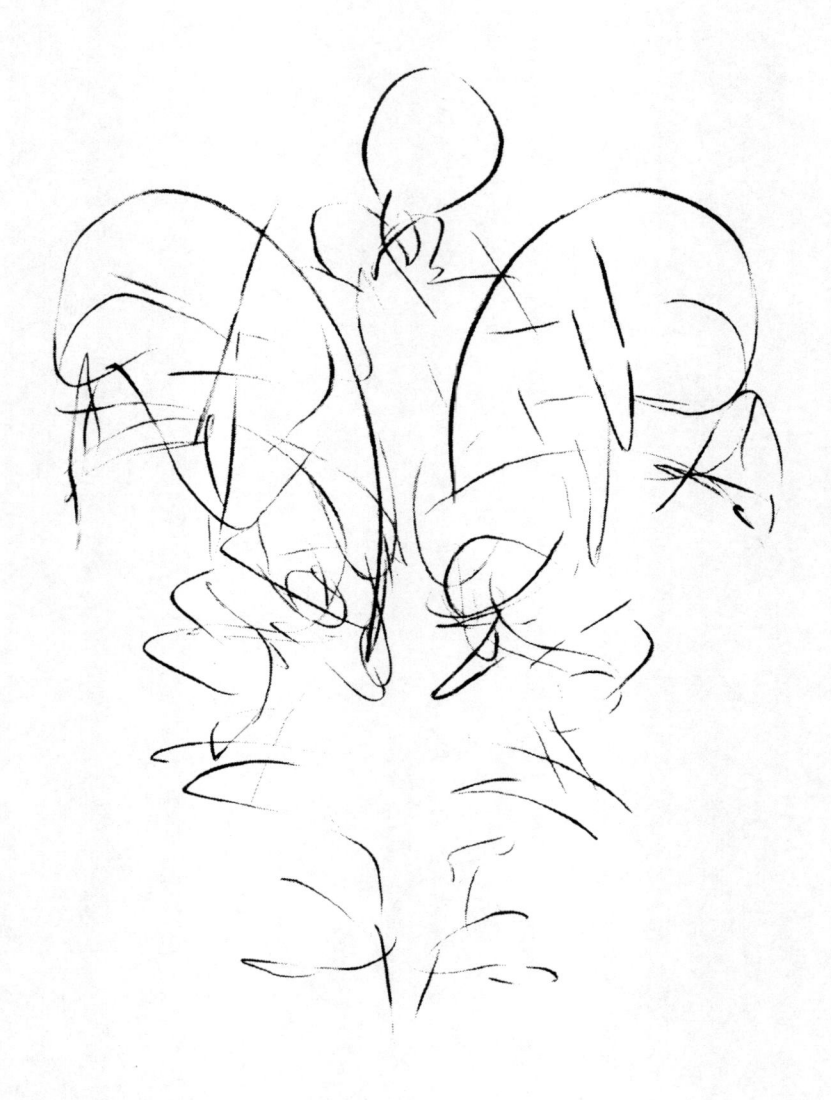

Spirit Rising, 2017, charcoal on paper, 22 x 30 inches

10

Spirit

Ancient tarot says ten can transform us.
Ten, the holiest of numbers: being
and non-being; matter and spirit; ten.
God smote Egypt with ten plagues: blood, frogs, gnats,
flies, and wild animals attacking. Boils,
hail storms and flashing fire. Locusts covered
land, and darkness prevailed for three days.
All suffer when some are held captive. Ten.
Beat your breast or beat upon a drum: one.
Make a list of verbs: release, forgive, love.

Let go. Let life flow. Release to reach zero.
Odysseus took ten years to return
to Ithaca after he won the war.
Greeks used pebbles to form letters before
stylluses or parchment. Deca: formed from
pebbles stacked: four three two one and
then a triangle formed—made of ten small stones.
The strongest shape can still be shattered with ease.
It goes from existence to nothingness. Done.
Ten commandments handed to Moses.

If we lived by them, we would be at peace.
Earthquakes are measured in tenfold—
Seven point ones have ten times six's power.
The ancient church received the tenth child as
a tithe to god. Hildegard Von Bingen
was tenth born. Her visions and her music
transformed us. We each can be reborn, reborn.
Length of a hand equals one-tenth your height.
Proportion, perfection, propensity—
found and bound together in number ten.

Knowing, 2017, charcoal on paper, 30 x 22 inches

11

Knowing

11 dimensions exist composed of tiny vibrating strings,
jiggling and wiggling our universe to create cosmic shortcuts,
ripping and tearing across membrane and space
where god lives. God sends forth the 11
monsters of chaos—formless and infinite.
Who has the right to spurn them? Not I.
Not at this 11th hour with no Joseph in sight,
Joseph, the eleventh son. I cannot see a
multicolored dream coat. I cannot hear him speak.
How can he, when he has been charged
with the responsibility of interpreting a
new pharaoh sporting platinum hair?
I am one of those monsters, and so are you.
11 chairs are filled and
emptied as if we all are players in a game
of Upset-the-Fruit-Basket.
No one gets comfortable for long.
Listen. What are our degrees of freedom?
The ones we make. The ones we take.
The ones we defend. Tiny strings we cannot see create
vibrations. Are we listening to this quartet—
a bass, a cello, a viola,
and a violin—are we listening to ourselves?

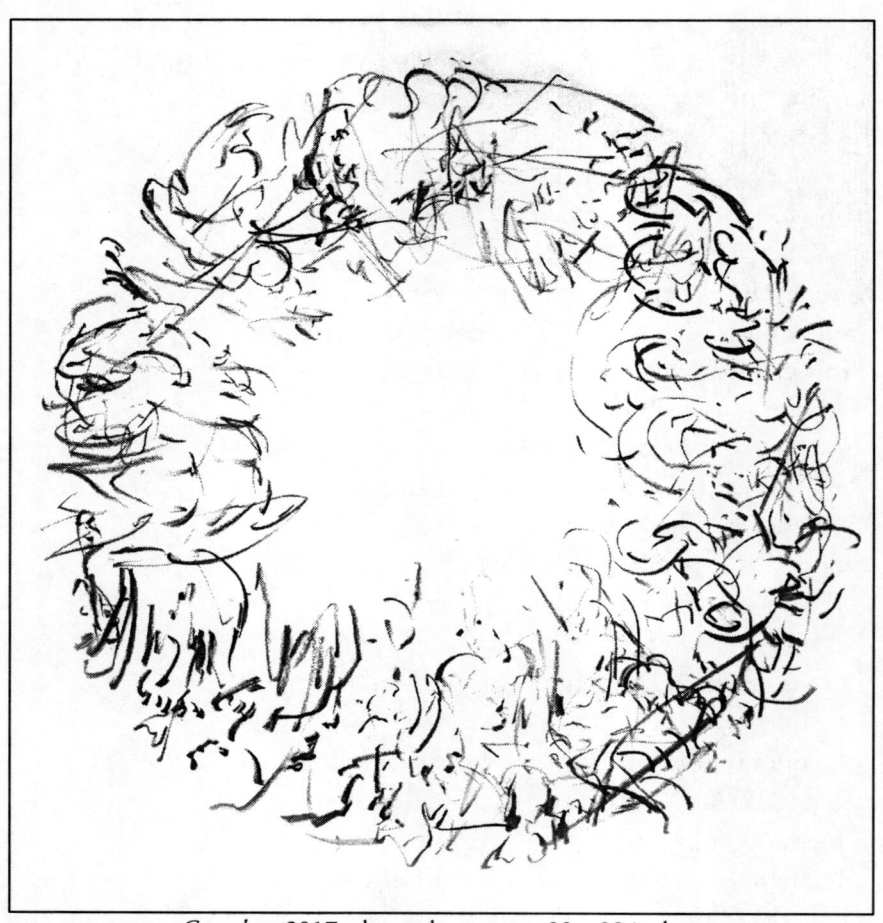

Complete, 2017, charcoal on paper, 22 x 22 inches

12

Complete

Twelve is the largest number with a single syllable name: 12 months, disciples, tribes, inches, signs of the Zodiac; a dozen eggs, cookies, rolls, notes in an octave which seems contradictory; 12 hours twice each day to live; 12 steps in AA, 12 days of Christmas, 12 cranial nerves in each of our heads; 12 knights at Arthur's roundtable, 12 sons for Odin, 12 people on a jury, hung or in agreement; 12 heavens where 12 legions of angels sing; 12 gates to the human body, 12 labors of Hercules, 12 people walked on the moon, and 12 is the number that manifests the Trinity. Eat 12 grapes as the clock strikes 12 on New Year's Eve to guarantee good fortune, after all 12 is the number of completion.

Did you catch all that? Could you take it all in? What does it mean? Why do we care? When the Israelites wandered in the wilderness, freed, they wore what clothes they had on their backs and waited for signs, orders, at least one epiphany—really wanting to be told what to do. Wear holy garments in beauty and glory, a voice told them, this is a part of a much longer story. Consecrate yourselves and the world, too, in gold and blue, scarlet and purple. Make the finest linen. Where do you find fields of flax in a desert? Engrave a giant onyx with all the names you know or can imagine, leave some space for edits and additions. Now here's the hard part, as if the rest were possible. Make a breastplate of judgment or several thousands. Teach the people who wander to wear them over their hearts, at home or in exile, at home or in exile.

Or imagine the desert of your own life, while you await your exodus' conclusion. You look around the place where you dwell, a little bit of heaven and a little bit of hell. If you opened up your space as an embassy for god, what artifacts would you would need for the job? What would you keep, and what would you discard? Assume you have no linen or breastplates or onyx. What then? Oh, there's a chipped platter, an old blanket chest, a chopping block with a loose leg that's propped. On the windowsill you feature an abandoned robin's nest you found with one broken egg and a yolky mess. You wonder about proportion and atmosphere, clouds and the sea, spirits and caves, and rooms full of assumptions with no space for questions.

II.

Breathing

As the model twists her torso, raises her arm, drops her waist, turns her head, and transfers her weight, I draw. Sensing energy and strain, I record the wake of the body as it flows through space. I contemplate the imprint of the gesture; then erase the unnecessary to reveal the essential.

-Patricia Brown

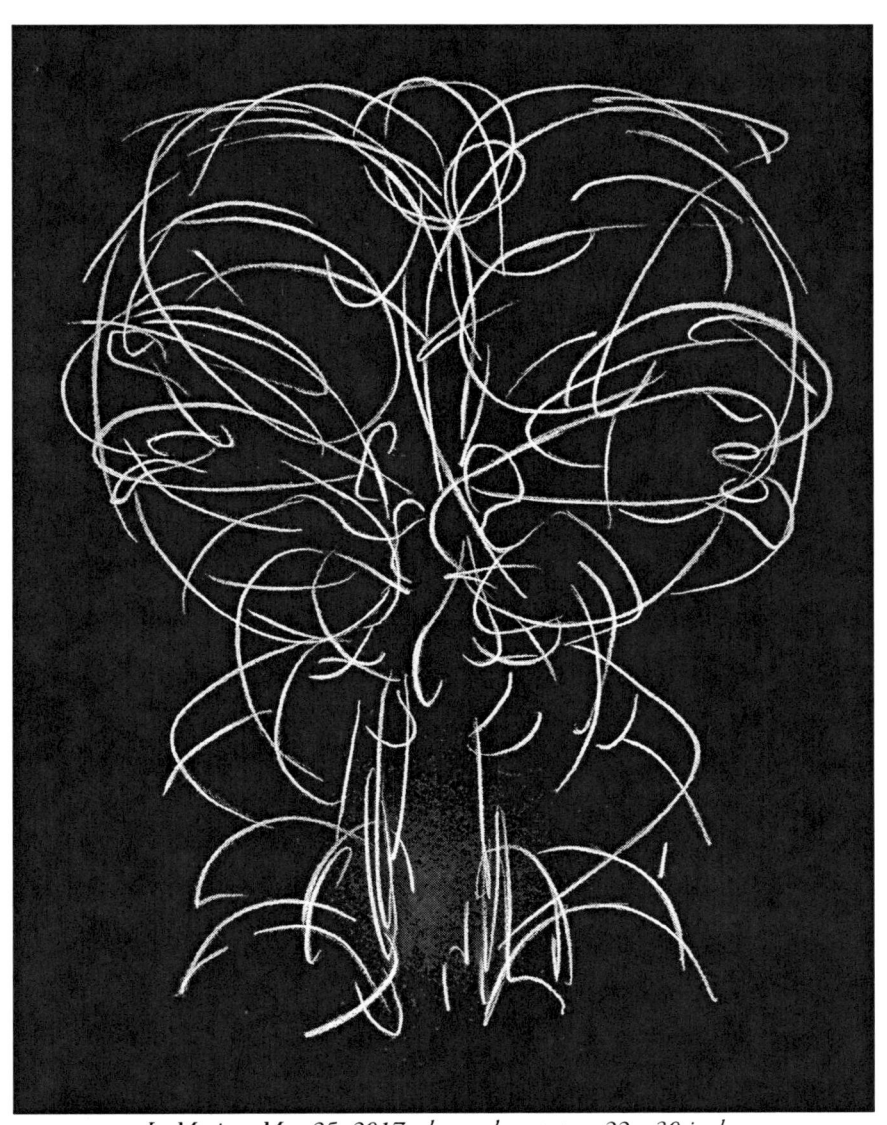

In Motion, May 25, 2017, charcoal on paper, 22 x 30 inches

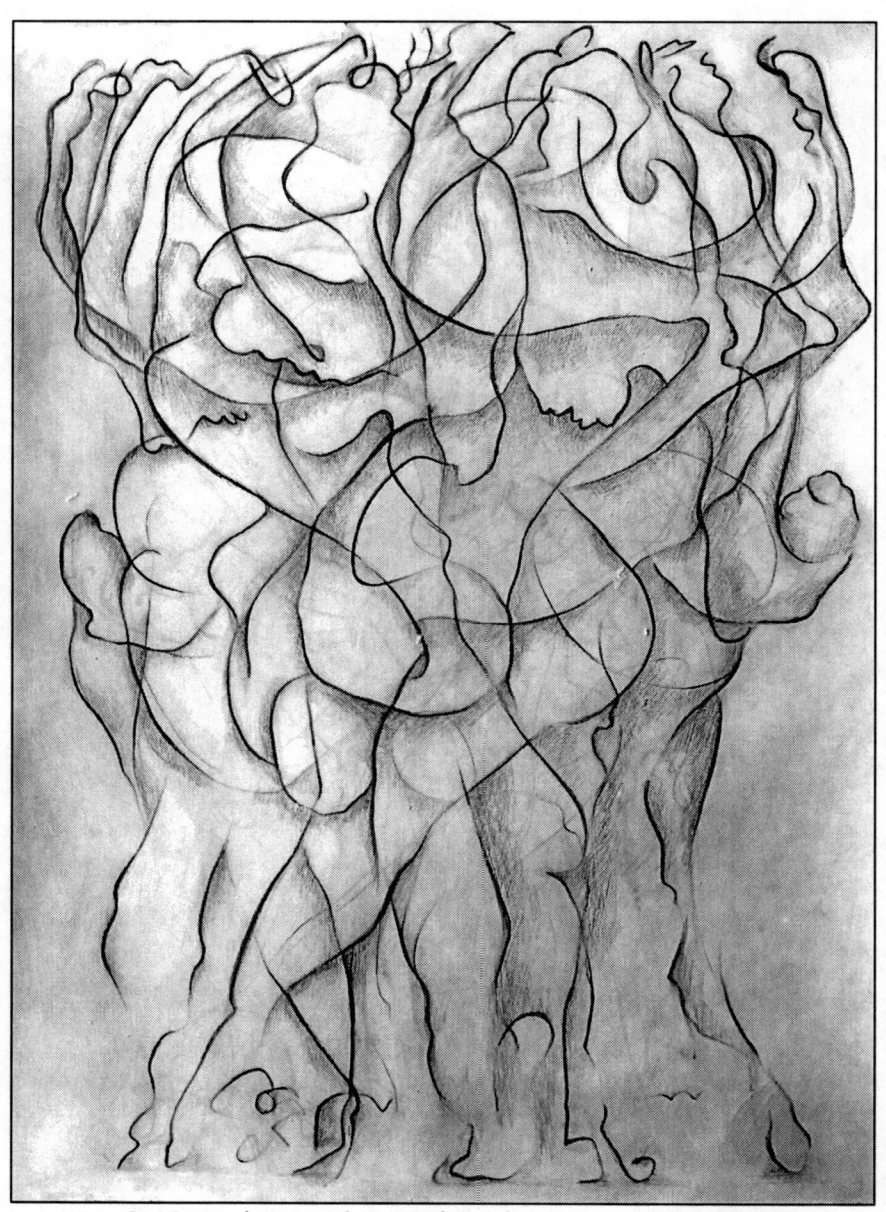

In Motion 4, August 4, 2016, charcoal on paper, 22 x 30 inches

In Motion, August 5, 2016, acrylic on canvas, 36 x 41 inches

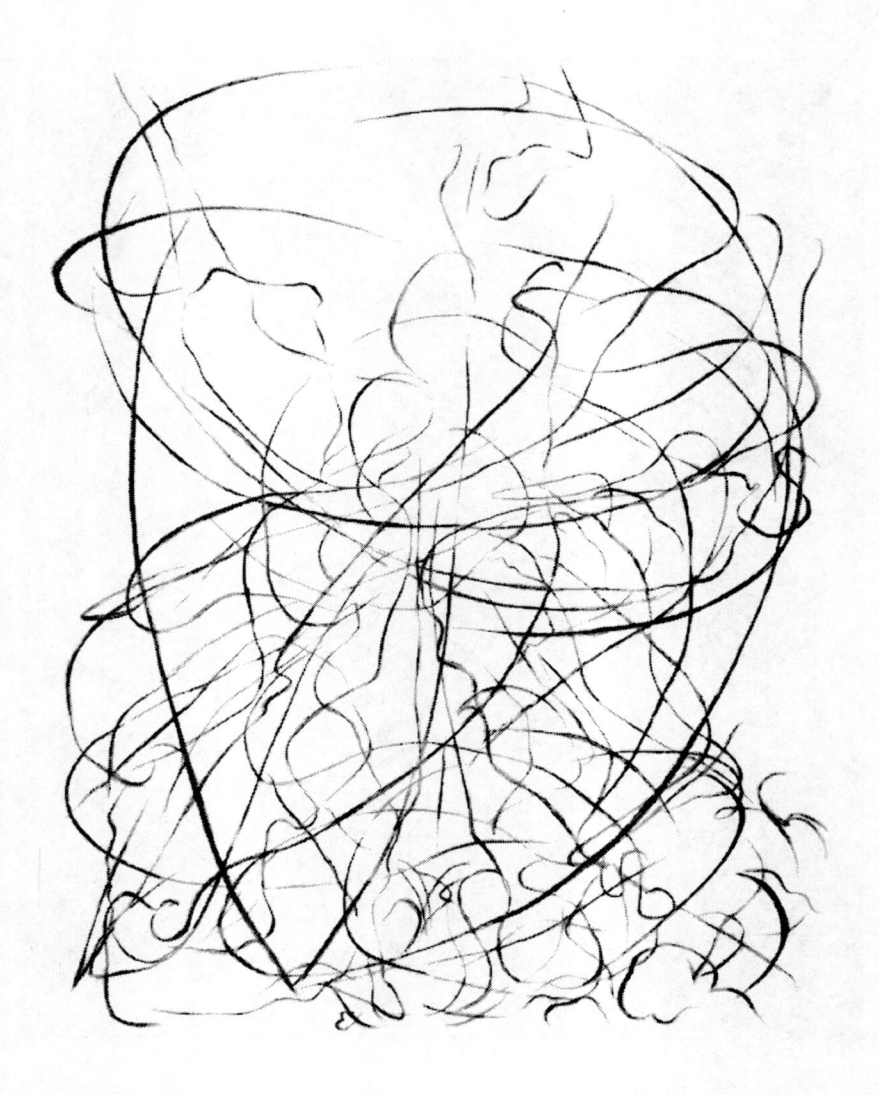

In Motion 2, November 1, 2016, charcoal on paper, 22 x 30 inches

In Motion, November 5, 2016, acrylic on canvas, 36 x 41 inches

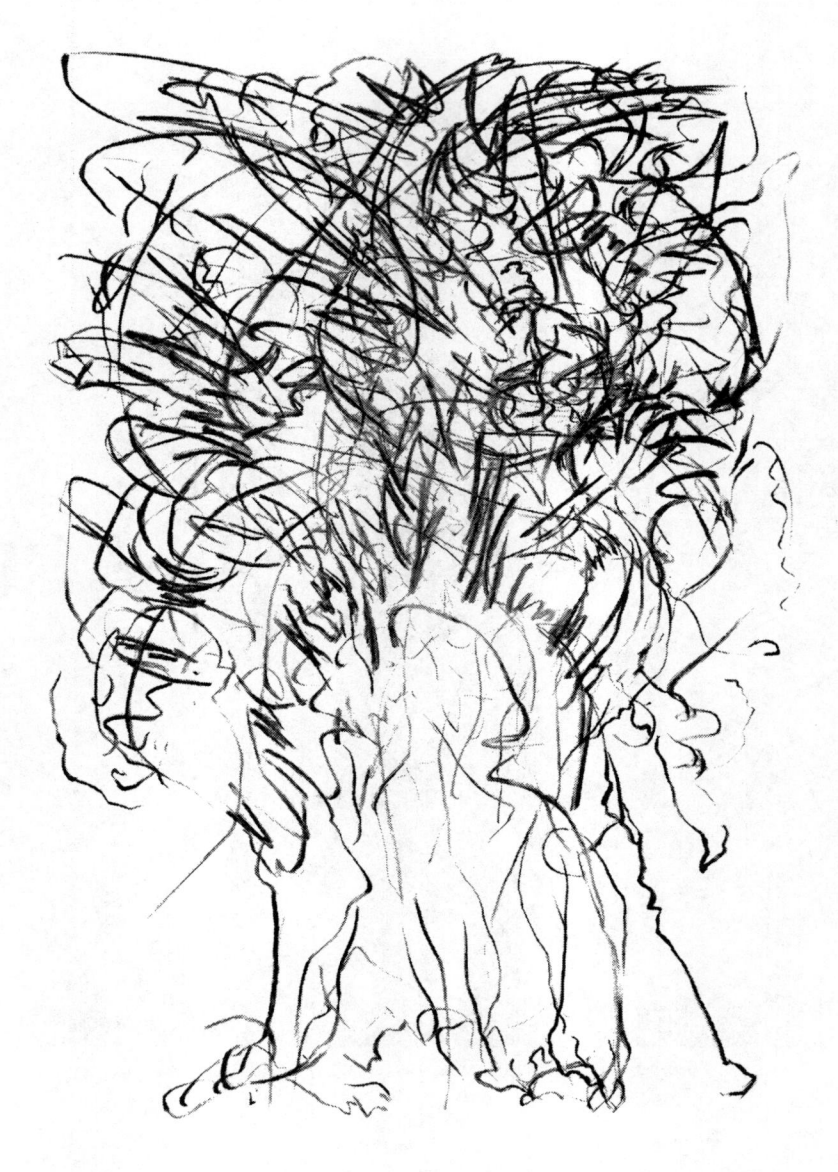

In Motion 3, April 22, 2017, charcoal on paper, 22 x 30 inches

In Motion, March 4, 2017, acrylic on canvas, 30 x 44 inches

In Motion2, April 21, 2017, charcoal on paper, 22 x 30 inches

In Motion, March 15, 2017, acrylic on canvas, 24 x 30 inches

III.
Seeking

Holding Half

I.

The record of things you have known.
The written language is a silenced echo
in an epigram, an image. Kissed cheek,
the hand brushing the shoulder. Each stance
a posture in flesh, in marble, in air.
The written language is cut into the veins of the hand.
The fingertips touch the head and in the space made
a bird is caged, sings flat through closed beak.
Place the written words in a sequence.
No key signature opens the cage.
The written language forgets to breathe.
It grows hair; nails grow while the skin dies.
Words follow word. A dripping faucet no one fixes.
The long line of people you've loved.
Gone searching in its ripeness. Gone bad in the bitter.

II.

Food matters; money matters; sleep matters.
The tight thighs that rock me
in the cradle of your hips matter.
Pink flesh on pink, matters.

There's no sameness in desire:
sweaty arms, pristine slope of fresh
shaved cheek, the hollow silence of hurt.
Petroleum soaks your jeans; oil frames
bitten nails, outlines the callous.
Love's slow twisted sheet lies
at the foot of the bed.

Pale face of a Hugenout, placid green eyes
impervious to my taunts.
Long fingered hands feed deer,
pick my fruited nipples, hold our daughter.

Snores percolate, force me to torture you
awake where I dwell watchful of Death.
What if I say or do the wrong thing to you,
you go to work and die before we can reconcile?
and the spirit, husband, will it hover
as I dream your arms around my waist,
Your smooth hard cock no longer
buried in my heat but limp under dirt
or burned to ash?

III.

This isn't a dream. This is a deck of cards.
And these are ideas about one of a kind
snowflakes, people, forms of torture.
How each thing is what it is named
and how language fails. We west, no north,
so south feast. Food unnamed still eaten.
Who knows each action from floss to churn
How the fat separates from meat and bone.
Larch masquerades as conifer without amber.
Twice nightly windows open and close,
through them, seen and not unseen, the mountain,
the city of god, a landfill, and a roulette wheel.

IV.

Foot and thumb are pressed in ink, recorded
to be traced. In that we are all similar.
Does the eye disintegrate before skin?
Dry and lose its color, the black pupil
snuffed and smoking? Tattooed skins with signatures
are preserved under glass but never eyes.
Oysters in a bag, touched in darkness
feel an eye removed. The body turns
into stone above ground; on plazas
the pigeons festooned in iridescent pinks
and greens shimmer gray, drop.
The cat bites down on rabbit head, chomps bone
but silent eats the eyes. Marbles holding
flowers upright preserve a slice of blue.

V.

Sweet silage and the snow. It comes to this:
the narrow knocking the shallow weeds.
Empty and full – the symphony of stones,
Sweep of season, bare cupboard. Marrowless
the bones lift into flight. Real impinges
on wish, collapses lungs as napalm flares.
Ignite a body or a bird nest. Each burns.
Sharp corners intersect at angel wings.
Metal musics from train whistles and pounded tracks.
Consequences of desire, word whispered by bees in ivy.
So different than the same hum if in your hair.

In This Moment
for Kathleen Deyo Brady Spence

Chicory arrives—a cushion for
pear and pecorino tart. Honey cuts
its bitterness, makes a perfect union.

Sunflowers burst forth from red clay,
their blooms joyous bright. Stand among
them and shine, the world commands.
Hold them to you like lovers.
We do. Later that night when I fall to sleep
I am blanketed by yellow.

Cobblestones still not worn flat.
Irregular, hot, rough—everywhere at once.
What they are not:
sand, oceans, grass, concrete, ice or snow.
Around the duomo, they are laid
in the pattern of stars.

Oleander, magnolia, olive trees and vineyards.
Gardenias, geraniums, cactus and cypress.
We negotiate the familiar in the unfamiliar.
Birds sing and we can name none of them, at first
and then, oh, a mourning dove, oh, there, a crow.

In a window, lace hangs, behind a partially
opened shutter—a couch, a lamp, two wine glasses.
A so blue sky makes me want to drink it.

A priest doubts transubstantiation. Is wine
truly the blood of Christ? Is the wafer his flesh?
Propaganda? Miracle? When he breaks the wafer,
blood spills onto the altar cloth, now framed
and hanging for 700 years.
Miracles explode metaphors. And we work words
to name what cannot be explained.

Hearts, old and young, want touch and words,
want laughter and tears, want dance and divinity
alive in the streets. Beggar woman lies sleeping
shoeless on cobblestones, weary from offering
to pray for us, tired of doubt.

A fig tree so full its boughs scrape the earth,
a landscape emptied by an earthquake,
fullness and emptiness everywhere at once.

Vast open land hosts silver leaved olive trees.
Vineyards grow, row on row. A rose bush marks
the end or the beginning of each. Creamy yellow,
sleepy pink, roses red like bloody ink,
white tipped with the slightest peach,
I reach and tap a thorn,
one drop of blood, such holy wine.

Synesthesia
for Sarah-Ruth

A moment exists as an orchard
exists as love rolling and thundering, a full room
and a world made of wetness and miles driven.
Then it comes, rain and a future, all in one
moment – wet, unregulated, necessary – sashaying
the way a moment exists in an orchard. Grapes
peaches olives – sweet right beside bitter,
and bees a thunderstorm of pollination.

A moment arrives as an I, oppressed and oppressing, falls
to her knees and rises up again. A dashing dropping rhythm
of rain, and then seasons change.

She stands in a gorge with snowflakes landing
on her daughter's long lashes her coat her hat her hair.
Deep love, a peach pit, where the snowflake in its precision
and its singularity are her – it comes – snow love lashes.

Salt and Light ~ A Covenant

I.
Evil, like most things, takes time to grow—
small steps taken and subtle masks worn,
nudges and whispers, a wink and a laugh,
a slow poison can remain undetected, at first.
We feed ourselves before we feed others,
and that's bad manners. So we share.

Evil gets bigger and juicier still, until it startles us.
We don't want to believe it has arrived:
a knock on the door, a vehicle in the drive,
unanswered phone calls, a missed holiday,
then two, then five, more subtle than gunshots,
or fists, or knives—they come later, if needed,
so nothing can thrive.

A step-mother holds a 6 year old's hand
over the open flame of the stove and watches and smells
flesh burn. The father says he knew nothing
at all—denial an evil as sure as all others.
A government observes, like clinicians,
while thousands of citizens flee
on the ocean in boats not seaworthy, and
the world watches, too, as the bodies are dragged
to the shores of freedom—breathless.
That's how evil arrives—buried in silence,
packaged in lies, it moves right in and destroys lives.
Innocuous, at first, except the weight of it's atomic—
a slow poisoning of leeched radioactivity.

We nurse a grudge, refuse to forgive,
and deliver the truth with a bit of spin.
We twist a story that could be a win
until it is inside out and ugly as sin.
We refuse love. We prefer what's hard—
being alone and miserable with No Trespass signs
in our yards. The longer we do it, the more we are marred.
We justify, defend, and pretend we are guiltless
while we teach others the power of absence.
We tell part of the story, and we appear hurt and sad,
when really, quite honestly, we've gone utterly mad.

II.
So she casts her lot, seeking
an auspicious day to wage war
on evil, and its extended family:
there are at least six more.
She purchases a navy
and gray backpack with zippers and snaps,
two small pockets and one larger one in the back.

If she keeps the virtues separate,
she will not have enough spaces for each, so
she considers what to carry and what else she must leave.
I only need water, she thinks to herself, and so she begins
to pack nothing else, no object that is.
Restraint goes in first, god knows, she'll need that,
and courage is next with fortitude in a pouch.
Justice goes in one of the smaller pockets.
She believes that's all right:
it usually starts small, and then the situation grows it.

The clothing she wears is woven with prudence—
large in its spread of controlled expectations.
She makes a checklist of rules to review at each dawn:
> Avoid unnecessary dangers;
> Be wise and use reason, regardless of weather,
>   regardless of season;
> Conserve resources of every kind;
> Apply skill and will and don't lose your mind.

Lying beside the pouch on her bed? Faith, hope and love.
Where do they go with their wonder and wisdom?
She considers putting them in her head, already too full
of rhymes and beliefs. So instead
she stuffs them and presses them and whacks them in place,
until she can fasten the buckle at last.

The backpack is amazingly light, the sun has arisen,
and she's eaten her omelet made from egg whites and spinach.

III.
It starts with a scapegoat. How could it not? You have to blame
    someone,
they have to be caught, doing something, anything, a thing you
    don't like,
and then you've got them and the viciousness starts.
Mordecai, from the Bible, refused to bow down to Haman,
    in Persia.
He believed in the commandments that said not to bow
before graven images of sheep, men or cows.
And gracious, good heavens that caused quite a stink,
one disobedient Jew, what might other people think?
So Haman concluded the best thing to do was kill all of them,
not leave one living Jew. Esther, Mordecai's niece and his ward,
caught wind of the plot and told it all to King Xerxes, right
    quick.

Xeres had picked Esther from among a lot
of beautiful women and made her his queen,
and she convinced him that killing all Jews was just mean,
plus she admitted with frankness and grace, when you look at
    me,
Xerxes, you are looking at a Jewish face.
(Adolf Hilter was a proponent as well,
kill and recycle was part of his cure
for a country so dominated by fear,
that it followed his orders and gave up free will--
but that's a different century, may he burn in Hell.)

IV.
She is wondering how she will save herself,
and perhaps, a small piece of the world, from evil.
Phrases come into her mind from her upbringing:
Are you worth your salt?
Your grandmother is the salt of the earth.

Why salt? She does her research:
Each cell in our bodies contains salt.
Get a basket and go to the sea, strain the water to gather
salt, garnered in the old way;
this salt is never used in cooking. Instead it is reserved
for sprinkling on food. Taste what it does,
how it activates the flavor, all the while it keeps the signals
    operating
in the brain—to and from, within and without.

Ethiopian salt is white gold. Bar, after bar, after bar.
India mixes its salt with harad seeds, turns it black,
then grinds it into pink powder.
The Japanese threw it on the stage
to prevent evil spirits from entering the actors.
Travel to the Bolivia and go to Salar de Uyuni—

4000 square miles of a salt flat that make a mirror
for scientists. And light? Where would we be without it?

Can you carry the light? Can you find a place
where the light gets in? The crack? The groove?
The cut in the velvet sky where the already dead star
shines through? Am I worth my salt? The young woman
with her striped backpack wonders.

V.
So she packs salt and a flashlight, three candles and some
    matches.
She sleeps one more time in her bed, and then she is off, out
    the door,
down the walk, toward the shore. She is armed with what she
    thinks matters:
some light and some salt and the virtues that clatter like dishes
    not wrapped
quite properly, in the backpack she carries.
                                      What's clear and clearer?
What's near and nearer? What's dear and dearer? What's fear?
    What's fear?

She wants to repair what is broken, mend what is torn, build
    back what has fallen,
and sing songs of love. Fighting evil feels heavier than bricks
    of salt,
and more elusive than light. But it is her mission, her
    responsibility, her right.
She will say less and mean more; she will guard the weak and
    help the poor,
she will question the foolish, including herself, and she will
    laugh often, of course.
Fighting evil cannot be all work and no play. She knows there's
    a lot to do in a day.

She will choose wisely which battles to fight, and when it gets dark,
she will carry the light. She'll wrap pain in love, smother fear with faith,
and send missives of hope to the whole human race. Salt and light support her.
Salt and light are her friends. She will share them; she will give them away;
and receive them as needed at the end of the day.

Extravagant Mercy

For every action there is a cost:
sensible things, limits, gushing love,
and all the grief of the world, a bitter frost.

She used almost a year's wages to buy
oil from India. She carried it in her waistband.
When he arrived, she doused his feet,
her hair a towel in a limited world.

For every action there is a cost
and a host of opinions about motives and truth.
Judgments are made and visions lost.

She lost her head and squandered the money,
forgetting boundaries and practical work.
Her heart ruled her head and she sang love,
and she sang forgiveness like the blues.

For every action there is a cost,
arise and arrive at pulsating grace,
and leave retaliation in the dust.

She broke open her heart to death
and let the sweetness pour out, second by second.
She smuggled infinity into the world,
multiplying zero with each breath.

Mending

Clothes lay in a basket at the foot of the stairs,
waiting to be repaired. If grace is the thread,
what is the needle? Or is grace the needle,
and we are the thread? Her heart is a sewing basket
filled with every color of thread,
the sharpest scissors, the straightest pins.
We each hold a needle up
to the graying yellow light coming through
a northern window, north—the direction of dreams.

Bridges traverse creeks, streams, rivers and seas.
Built to last, repaired as needed. If love is a bridge,
then what is the water? Or if love is the water,
then who needs a bridge? He puts on a swimsuit.
He uses the bridge to launch toward the water,
south--the direction of beginnings.

Birds soar into another body of blue.
If hope is a pair of wings,
where does it fly? Or if hope is flight,
what keeps us from soaring? Robins, sparrows,
hawks and grosbeaks know from the beginning
who they are and from whence they come.
We sometimes forget, or some of us never knew.
When we go to deep remembering, we know
who we are, where we are from, and to whom we belong.

If faith is a map, where does it lead?
Or if faith is a location, how do we know when we have arrived?
We awaken from a dreamless sleep,
a place of deep forgetting—a cavern, a cave, a mountain peak.
We choose to remember or forget:

who we are, who we have been, who we are becoming.
We can be lost, and we can be found.
Pick up the sewing basket with all its thread,
and sew yourself back into the fabric.

Practice

All the wasted years before you,
before I knew how to fold a pillow in half,
lengthwise, in order to read comfortably
on my back in bed: the years troubled by lack
of air, before I knew athletes, especially
runners, breathe best through
their noses and their mouths.

The certain thick possibility of separation:
How I send myself away to make certain
I will know how to breathe, eat, walk, sleep
when you are gone, as if practice will help
when I lose you.

My strident language filled with image and story
met most often by your voice saying: The truth
lies somewhere in between the two extremes.

Ways to use a body, and use, you say, is not bad.
What good, you say, is it to be of no use?
What good, indeed. Ski, swim, move out, move in.
and with you there is our baby – human, dolphin, angel:
coded by all I do not understand to come from us
but past us – parts identifiable – the whole unknown, not yet
revealed, observing miracles so closely –
then almost gone. We embrace our reprieve, life, her.

Sometimes I see a world as it is
with you in it, but I am gone – riveted
to a star – some cold thing of aging stone.
From it I watch you move as you move
now, but without me moving out of your way.
You no longer have to move your shoes or the news-
paper, or eat cups and cups of vegetables,
buy two kinds of dental floss, no longer
have to tell stories, argue about fear,
wrestle me into doing things I resist and love.
My absence is not a relief as I suspected,
as I hoped, as I feared. Instead I hear you
missing me in the soughing echo of tree limbs.
All the practice will do no good
in preparing us for absence.

Raw
for Jeff

i.

A lightning rod protects the barn
creating a low resistant path to ground—
without allowing fire, but seeking, seeking
a safe way down. The route is obvious once known.

ii.

I catch, hold, throw zig-zagged lightning bolts,
gold and sharp. Grabbed from the center
of the cyclone I have entered.
I drink liquid glass, inhale and exhale
wind, dust myself with dirt,
and wear a ring of fire—
dancing to what I hope is not the last dance.

iii.

Wind feeds the soul of trees.
Without it, no whispering pines,
no rustling leaves—instead,
silent and caged, trees hold their souls erect.
Each tree would remain alone without wind.
Underground a root might cross, but there is no guarantee.

iv.

Scarves receive purpose from the wind:
warming necks, holding chins, caressing hair.
Wind insists and scarves sometimes succeed and sometimes fail.

v.

Fire water burns as it goes down.
Beneath sky, under ground, within these depths,
I begin. 100 spinning atoms float without and within.
I choose the closet of love to live in with you.
I shatter patterned windows and let
white light, screaming wind, cooling water, and you,
my earth, in.

Lisa Harris writes poetry, short fiction, and novels. Her poetry has been published in journals such as, *The Penman, Puerto del Sol, Vending Machine Press, The Coe Review, ginosko* and *descant*. Her novels, *Geechee Girls, Allegheny Dream*, and *The Raven's Tale* comprise *The Quest Trilogy* (2013, 2014, 2017, Ravenna Press). She lives and writes in the Finger Lakes region of New York.

Patricia Brown creates drawings, paintings, collages and mixed media assemblages. Her artwork has been shown in venues such as the Spool Factory, Russell Sage College Gallery, Forman Gallery, Yeager Museum, Impact Gallery, Center Way Gallery, WomanMade Gallery and the Cooperstown Art Association. She is an artist member of State of the Art Gallery in Ithaca, NY. She lives and creates in the Finger Lakes region of New York.

Credits: Thanks to the following journals and magazines who have published Lisa Harris' poems: Counting, "Zero," "One," "Four," and "Seven" in *The Penmen Review*, Southern New Hampshire University; "Eight," *ginosko;* "Holding Half," *Puerto del Sol;* "Synthesia," *The Second Word Thursdays Anthology;* "Salt and Light," *Vending Machine Press;* "Extravagant Mercy," *Cayuga Lake Books;* "Raw" and "Mending," *Facets;* "Practice," *Stillwater*.

Thanks to the State of the Art Gallery, Ithaca, NY, for exhibiting Spirit, House, Shalom and the In Motion Series, April 2017.

ACKNOWLEDGEMENTS

Both the author and artist's work have received support from The Constance Saltonstall Foundation in Ithaca, NY.

Patricia Brown's work benefitted from energetic collaboration with models, Vanessa Prouix and Jamie Warburton. Her approach to drawing has been greatly influenced by artists Tim Hawkesworth and Lala Zeigland.

EQIS Fin. Ins
WED 8PM
Bill LAMPE
940 465 0042

712 775.7270
101291#